Sukkot Treasure Hunt

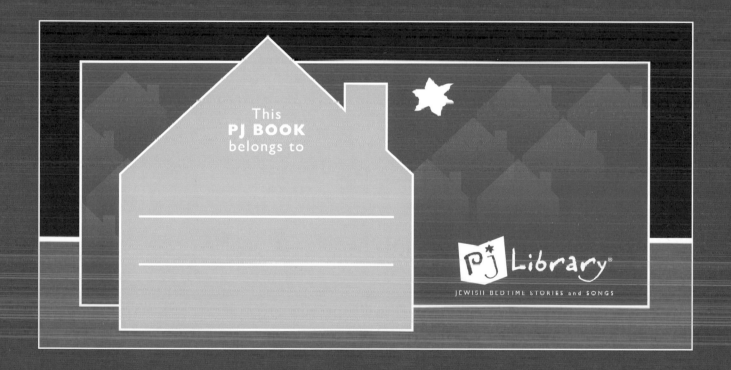

This **PJ BOOK** belongs to

PJ *Library*®
JEWISH BEDTIME STORIES and SONGS

By Allison Ofanansky
Photos by Eliyahu Alpern

KAR-BEN
PUBLISHING

To my parents, Martin and Cecily Slater, for all their love and support.
— A.O.

To Yagel, Aravah, Billy, Elijah, Noah, Ethan, and all the other children:
it's better to find the stuff on your own. Get in touch with your world!
— E.A.

Fun Facts Acknowledgments: Krispil, Nissim (1988). *A Bag of Plants: The Useful Plants of Israel.* Arad: Yara Publishing House. *The Encyclopedia of the Plants and Animals of Israel.* Jerusalem: Society for the Protection of Nature in Israel. Thanks to Dr. Yossi Leshem of Tel Aviv University for eagle identification.

Kar-Ben Publishing
A division of Lerner Publishing Group, Inc.
241 First Avenue North
Minneapolis, MN 55401 U.S.A.
1-800-4-KARBEN

Website address: www.karben.com

Library of Congress Cataloging-in-Publication Data

Ofanansky, Allison.
    Sukkot treasure hunt / by Allison Ofanansky ; photographs by Eliyahu Alpern.
        p.   cm.
    Summary: In Israel, a young girl and her family go on a scavenger hunt to find the "four species" they will use in their celebration of the Jewish holiday, Sukkot. Includes facts about plants named in the story.
    ISBN 978-0-8225-8763-7 (lib. bdg. : alk. paper)
        [1. Sukkot—Fiction. 2. Treasure hunt (Game)—Fiction. 3. Jews—Fiction. 4. Israel—Fiction.] I. Alpern, Eliyahu, ill. II. Title..
    PZ7.O31Suk 2009
    [E]—dc22   2008031202

Manufactured in China
1-43875-33939-3/14/2017

091720.8K1/B1088/A7

Abba (that's my dad)
holds a wooden board
while I hammer in the nails.
We are building a sukkah
in our yard. Sukkot will
begin in a few days.

I help Ima (that's my mother) hang curtains around the frame to make the walls. Abba and I carry leafy branches to pile on top for the roof. I hang decorations to make our sukkah beautiful.

We are almost ready. But we still need the "four species."
Every morning of Sukkot we will hold these four plants
together and wave them up, down, and around. I learned
about the four species in school. They are:

the *lulav*—a branch from a date palm, bound with . . .

aravot, branches from a willow tree

and *hadas,* myrtle, which has nice-smelling leaves.

The fourth is the *etrog* which looks like a big lemon.

Before Sukkot, lots of people sell them from stands set up on the streets in cities throughout Israel.

But we're not going to buy them in a market. We're going on a treasure hunt to see if we can find them where they grow in the hills and valleys near Tzefat where we live.

A fat, furry rock rabbit called a hyrax watches us as we hike down into a valley. When we get closer, he scurries behind a thorn bush.

I see a tree with shiny leaves, small berries, and a nice smell. Could it be the myrtle? Ima shakes her head. "It's a bay leaf tree," she says. We pick a few leaves anyway—to put into soup.

Here is the myrtle! I take a big sniff of the spicy scent. We search through the patch until we find the most perfect branches. Abba helps me cut some. We put them in the backpack and continue on our treasure hunt.

We have found one of the four species!

Something red and purple catches my eye. "Look at that," Abba says, "a grapevine climbing up a pomegranate tree." He picks some of each. "Sukkot is a harvest holiday and we should enjoy all the fruits that are ripe now."

As we get further down in the valley, I hear water flowing. Lots of trees grow near the water. As we go closer we see a willow! Its leaves are long and narrow. Its thin branches bend easily, and I carefully cut a few. I wet a towel in the creek, and we wrap the delicate willow with the myrtle to keep them fresh.

Now we have two of the four species!

We are getting hungry, so we eat lunch by the creek.
We have sandwiches from home and fruits we collected
on our treasure hunt. My favorite is the pomegranate.
After lunch I take off my shoes and wade in the warm,
shallow water.

"We'd better get going if we are going to find a lulav and an etrog," Abba says. We pack up our picnic and head out again.

Look at this tree! Is that an etrog?

No, it's a little wild orange. Yuck, it's bitter!

Still no etrog.

We start to climb up out of the valley. I see an eagle sitting at the top of a tall tree. It takes off and flies away, looking for something to eat. Maybe it sees an etrog tree.

The sun is getting low over the hills. We take a bus
back home.

There are other people on the bus carrying lulav and
etrog bundles.

I am tired from the long walk, but my tummy is full of all the
fruits we ate, and I'm happy we found all the four species
on our Sukkot treasure hunt.

Chag Sameach!

Happy Holiday!

FUN FACTS about the species mentioned in this book:

Etrog: The etrog was the first citrus fruit to grow in the Middle East. It has grown there for over 3,500 years—since the time of Abraham.

Lulav (date palm): The honey of the "land of milk and honey" is not from bees—it is a syrup made from the date fruits. The date palm has been called a "tree with no waste." Aside from giving us tasty fruits and the lulav, the stems can be used to weave beautiful, strong baskets, and the leafy fronds can be used for shade (such as the roof of a sukkah).

Arava (willow): Willow bark has long been used to cure headaches and fevers— it contains the same type of chemical used to make the first aspirin (salicin).

Hadas (myrtle): Sometimes at traditional Jewish weddings, guests dance before the bride and groom with branches of myrtle, so they can enjoy its beautiful smell. Oil made from myrtle can also be used as an insect repellant.

Bitter oranges: These citrus fruits are too bitter to eat, but they are the "parent" of many citrus fruits we eat, like oranges and grapefruits. Israel grows and exports many citrus fruits, such as Jaffa oranges. All citrus fruits are high in vitamin C. The Hebrew word for citrus *(hadar)* means "splendid" or "wonderful."

Bay leaves: Bay leaves are used in soups and stews. In ancient times, branches of some kinds of bay leaves, also called "laurel," were woven into crowns and worn to show status.

Hyrax: These little "rock rabbits" live in very dry places and can live without drinking water. They get enough moisture from the plants they chew up. They can eat plants which are poisonous to many other animals.

Short-toed eagle: This large bird sits high in trees or hovers, almost still in the air, until it spots its prey—a snake. The eagle can eat snakes up to 6 feet long (2 meters) and can even eat poisonous snakes, but once in awhile the snake wins and kills the eagle.

ABOUT SUKKOT

Sukkot (The Festival of Booths) recalls the temporary huts the Jewish people built as they wandered in the desert after the Exodus from Egypt. The autumn holiday is also a celebration of the harvest. Jewish families build and decorate sukkot outside their homes and synagogues and eat their meals there. They may also study and read in the sukkah and even sleep there on warm nights. As a symbol of the harvest, the Torah commands us to "take the branches and fruit of beautiful trees and rejoice." The "four species" used are the palm, willow, myrtle, and etrog.

ABOUT THE AUTHOR

Allison Slater Ofanansky, born in the USA, became an Israeli citizen in 1996. She lives in the village of Kaditah, near the mystical city of Tzefat, with her husband Shmuel and their daughter Aravah. They all enjoy hiking in the hills of the Galilee, gathering and eating the fruits that grow there. Together they are involved in environmental and "eco-peace" projects. Allison is a graduate of Syracuse University with a degree in journalism, and works as an editor of academic articles and books. She is also the author of the children's book *Harvest of Light* (Kar-Ben).

ABOUT THE PHOTOGRAPHER

Born and raised outside Chicago, Eliyahu (Andrew) Alpern has been interested in food, travel, and photography since early childhood. He has cultivated his creative expression through many professions – musician, cougar rehabilitator, vegetarian chef, organic farmer, web designer, tour guide, and multimedia maven. Eliyahu lived in Michigan, Oregon, Colorado, Jerusalem, and New York before settling in Tzefat. Specializing in 360-degree panoramic images of Israel, Eliyahu's work offers a unique perspective on the country, including holy sites, markets, and natural vistas. Eliyahu shares his life and home with his wife Nili, son Yagel, cat Slick, and dog Sanchez. For more of his art visit www.tziloom.com.